A journey to self-discovery

LOVE AND LIGHT

MANTRA CARDS

Ali Oetjen and Marion Piret

INTRODUCTION

· ◐ ● ◑ ·

Welcome, if you're looking to find a profound source of positivity and guidance the universe has delivered these hand-illustrated cards just for you. Designed to illuminate your path with love, wisdom, and enlightenment, each card carries the power to uplift your spirit, offer insight and remind you that love and light are always within reach. Whether you seek motivation, solace, or simply a daily dose of inspiration, these cards are your companions on the journey to a brighter, more fulfilling life. Embrace their radiant messages and let them infuse your days with hope, encouragement and the enduring warmth of love and light.

Ali Oetjen

How to use the cards

To use these cards effectively, draw one daily. Recite the powerful mantra to affirm its message, read the card's description for insight and embrace the suggested action to reinforce healing and wisdom. Let each card guide your day and empower your journey towards love and light.

THE CARDS

1. THOUGHTS BLOSSOMING INTO REALITY

Take note of where your energy is going, being specific with your thoughts, language and actions as they're creating your next moment, your biggest dreams. Your thoughts are like a magnet, attracting in what you're consistently thinking about. Make your thoughts purposeful and positive and have them be in alignment with your deepest desires.

Action: write down one thought you'd like to implement in your daily routine that will positively change your life. Keep it by your bedside to remind you every day until it becomes habit and your life is changed!

2. BE LOVE

Accept your journey as ever unfolding, enhancing your life through experiences that lead to growth. Acknowledge that to hold the highest frequency of love, to give and receive love, you must first connect with your inner world and heart.

Action: bow your head and repeat 'I am love' three times. Rest your thumbs on your lips and repeat 'I speak loving words' three times. Press softly on your third eye with your thumb pads and repeat 'I think loving thoughts' three times.

3. FREEDOM IN TRUTH

What resistance, attachments and judgements can you let go of to feel free? Placing restrictions on any relationship, experience or circumstance leaves no room for flow and allows for disappointment. Set yourself free: there are lessons about you, an opportunity to deepen your relationship with yourself.

Action: do you feel freedom inside or outside your body? If it's inside, trust that when making future choices. If it's outside your body, ask yourself what is between you and your freedom?

4. BLISS IN PRESENCE

You never exist in the past or future: there is only now. Tune in to your senses and what you intuitively know with them. In these moments you will cultivate calmness that soothes your soul into being, into remembering this is what life is all about.

Action: search for the subtlest pieces of nature, for example, the nearly invisible veins in a leaf or the sound of ants moving, and spend 5 to 10 minutes immersing yourself in extreme detail with your senses. Come back with one smell, one touch, one sight and one sound.

5. FUTURE VISION

Look deep into your eyes and find the beauty within: stare at, recognise and honour it, and be proud. Reflect on your most profound moments, allowing them to resonate into your cells. Reflect on what may seem insignificant moments to truly understand you.

Action: look deep into your eyes without looking away for 1 minute and invite in a curiosity to deepen the love for you. Look past the exterior of your eyes and face for a further minute and start to feel your inner essence hug you.

6. RIDE THE WAVES OF LIFE

Do you feel as though you're invisible some days? Your light and love is always felt, so keep persevering and holding your vibration. Being a light warrior has its struggles, but you've been chosen because the natural radiance within you is needed.

Action: draw your breath in through your nose for four counts and send that breath into your heart space. Hold it for a second, then exhale for five counts through your nose and visualise clearing any cobwebs in your heart. Repeat for 2 minutes.

7. SELF-LOVE

Develop your self-esteem and confidence with encouraging words and self-love rituals. A natural desire to lift others up and become aware of their special traits and inner beauty will create a ripple effect, so find your inner spirit and let it start with you.

Action: turn the corners of your mouth up into a smile and remember how it feels when you tenderly take care of you. Implement one self-love practice today such as a bath, journalling your attributes or moisturising your body.

8. YIN AND YANG

Finding balance between your masculine and feminine energies can introduce more ease, safety and alignment in your life. Beneficial masculine traits include structured daily schedules and taking the lead, but they can be exhausting if feminine traits of connecting with your intuition, nurturing and allowing flow into your life aren't felt.

Action: play your favourite song and start moving your hips from side to side and wave your arms above your head. Feel into your heart while you sing and dance and surrender to the music returning you to balance.

9. BE THE CHANGE

Take note of every choice you make and ask yourself whether it is in alignment with your highest good and is good for the earth. Every choice matters: they will either allow the universe to deliver what is truly meant for you or deliver lessons that will steer you back into alignment. Your alignment is for the good of the universe.

Action: create one conscious choice that will positively impact the universe. To create space for this choice, also let go of a choice that isn't serving your highest good.

10. SHARE YOUR UNIQUENESS

Do what lights you up, taking note when you feel wild joy, gratitude and a knowingness in your body. This is a 'Yes' sign that you're doing exactly what you're designed to be doing. Distractions and negative influences will block the pain of ignoring your light, so don't settle for anything less than what enlivens you.

Action: journal what thrills you and do those things!

11. GROWTH

Life is always changing and you must change with it, sometimes more than you anticipated, but know in your heart that the universe always delivers what's meant for you at exactly the right time. You are exactly where you're meant to be.

Action: imagine a tree swaying in the wind and letting go of branches in strong winds to continue growing with new life. What immediately comes to mind that is keeping you from growing?

12. CHOOSE WITH YOUR HEART

Have you ever been faced with two choices that will lead you to two totally different lives? Listen to your heart and body when faced with these and know the right one will feel light and exciting with a hint of fear that only indicates the unknown. A full body 'Yes' will follow and put you on your way to your dreams. Your heart is your highest intuition.

Action: practise with smaller, insignificant choices such as a food preference or whether or not to go to an event. Honour what your heart tells you.

13. COMPASSION

Your power to feel deep compassion should be carefully navigated and your energy protected. It's important to connect often with yourself through mediation and stillness, which will best serve you to be the healer you are so you can help those in need rather than having your energy sucked from you.

Action: practise compassion with a person or animal in need, a loving understanding that secures your energy in place without putting yourself in their pain.

14. OVERCOME ADVERSITY WITH RESILIENCE

To learn and understand yourself and the universe, to reach your highest potential, you will be tested time and time again. How you show up and face those adversities makes you who you are. Always keep your character in check, stick by your morals and remember your values while being thankful in difficult times, which will ensure more ease and grace and cultivate inner strength and inspiration.

Action: write down your top five values in life. These could include health, family, romantic relationships, purpose, and so on.

15. CONNECT WITH NATURE

Have you heard Mother Nature calling you to her healing abode? It's been caring for you since you took your first breath, and shows you miracles, beauty, unwavering love and sacrifice. Take time out in nature to ground, feel and heal.

Action: take your shoes off and spend 5 minutes walking around on the earth exchanging energy with Mother Nature.

16. ABUNDANCE

You can be in an amazing relationship, enjoy optimum health, live an inspiring purpose, have an incredible lifestyle with time and freedom and be your true heart's desires. You can have it all: the only limits are the ones you create.

Action: be clear about what you want to create. Write it down and be it.

17. THAT IS WHAT YOU FEEL, SO THAT IS WHAT'S COMING

That which you are, you attract. Have you noticed when you're having a good day that more good things keep happening? Gratitude helps anchor you in the loving awareness of the universe, which is always taking care of you. Implement gratitude in your daily routine and watch how you gracefully power through.

Action: write down three things you're happy to have in your life and why those things give you joy.

18. VOLUNTEER AND SERVE

The more you help nourish the earth and beings that share it with you the better. Implement a new habit or task in your day, month or year that in no way benefits you. When you experience the gift of giving without expectations, the love that bubbles up in your heart is immeasurable.

Action: smile at three strangers who look like they really need it and hold no expectations for a return smile.

19. LISTEN

Are you listening to the things around you? When you listen you learn the most, about yourself, nature and your existence. When you truly listen you're able to hear true wisdom, and that absorbed wisdom is transformed into a greater awareness of your limitless potential.

Action: start by asking a question out loud to the universe and ask for it to send you a sign that you cannot miss.

20. LET GO

The now is all that exists. If you're having difficulty letting go, know that you never possessed anything in the first place. Fear is an energy that was never yours to claim, and worry is an energy that is simply passing through. There's no energy powerful enough to change the past.

Action: think about what you want to let go of. Close your eyes and visualise a cord running from you to it, then imagine cutting the cord and watching it slowly dissolve into nothing.

21. DREAM BIG

Dream bigger than you can imagine and believe without a doubt it's true, because those dreams are initiated with every action you take and ripple into giant waves that cross seas. The momentum of your dreams is felt by all that is, which speaks the language of energy and delivers that dream to you.

Action: create a vision board for your home and find pictures that represent your future dreams and creations such as house pictures, a romantic relationship or your purpose.

22. BE AN OBSERVER

Your perceptions are influenced by your life experiences and feelings and emotions. To be in a state of observation is an advanced and enlightened choice that incorporates all points of view, and therefore a greater level of understanding and awareness of the best outcome for your highest good.

Action: what do you struggle to perceive? What do you see when you zoom out or sense when you zoom in? What else don't you know yet? Be curious and ask yourself deep questions.

23. YOU ARE WORTHY OF IT ALL

It's time you spoke to yourself the way you lovingly speak to others. It's important to recognise your worth and express it openly and confidently.

Action: create a mantra to repeat to yourself out loud every morning as a daily ritual to practise self-love. Let this practise become a habit so it imprints in your beliefs and sets a standard of worthiness.

24. HEART-LED

Have you been thinking with your head? Instead, lead with your heart and change and adapt with its currents. This will allow your authenticity to shine and desires to be met. A heart-led life is an extraordinary, fulfilling, challenging life, and to feel it once is a sure sign you'll never deter from it.

Action: inhale for 5 seconds and exhale for 5 seconds with no pause. Practise this for 2 to 5 minutes.

25. LEAVE A LEGACY

Wherever you go you're leaving footprints. Have you been stepping purposefully? Remember that each step you take paves the way for others to follow, so the inspiration trail you leave behind is up to you.

Action: when you go to bed imagine your inspiration trail, what it looks like and what it feels like, as you drift off to sleep.

26. FEEL YOUR PURITY

Where your focus goes, energy flows. Does this resonate with your healing, work, purpose or relationships?

Action: create an intention in the morning and see your light and joy being shared. Enjoy every minute of where you focus on and feel its magnitude.

27. MAKE CURIOUSITY YOUR NATURE

Human beings have natural instincts to investigate the way things work, how they came to be and what they sense. Invite in more of your curiosity and question everything, as this is the way to find endless beauty.

Action: what is interesting you lately? Dive in, research and ask questions, and let your inquisitiveness run wild!

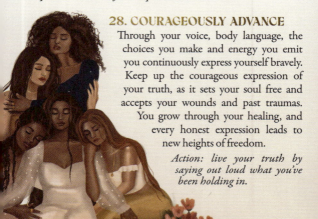

28. COURAGEOUSLY ADVANCE

Through your voice, body language, the choices you make and energy you emit you continuously express yourself bravely. Keep up the courageous expression of your truth, as it sets your soul free and accepts your wounds and past traumas. You grow through your healing, and every honest expression leads to new heights of freedom.

Action: live your truth by saying out loud what you've been holding in.

29. HONOUR

Stay true to who you really are. If the road seems difficult at times, come back to your heart and remember your reason why. Rekindle your connection with your heart and the honouring of your integrity.

Action: go and grab your favourite crystal and list three things about you that you're proud of.

30. TIME TO PLAY

Your love knows no bounds. Practise compassion more deeply for everything and you'll walk in a kinder world. The fun and care you give out will circle back to you tenfold.

Action: have fun today with a game of tag, climb a tree, throw a ball, roll around or play a board game.

31. DAILY HABITS

Have you got out of habit with your spiritual practices? Be gentle with yourself and know that you can never lose your spirituality. As with any belief, it's important to give it daily energy to keep the wisdom alive. How much time is it worth to enhance your life? Make space for the things that are important to you.

Action: enjoy your favourite spiritual practice today. If you don't yet have one, try a guided meditation.

32. CAST SPELLS WITH WORDS

The meaning you place upon anything is what you're creating. Be very specific about how you describe your days, moments and places: so specific in the way they make you feel, and so specific it turns them into the good you see in everything.

Action: go outside and look up at the sky, the clouds or stars and describe in detail your day so far, so much so that it brings it to life and gives it a sense of feeling.

33. BOUNDARIES

The way to safety, respect and honour is to create healthy boundaries, so other people are aware of your desires and so you protect your integrity and keep your word.

Action: practise creating a small boundary today, such as a food you won't eat or a place you won't go. Allow the small practice to grow into bigger boundaries that you lovingly share if need be.

34. WHAT IS

Don't get caught up in what ifs, as these are not in your reality and are created by a false story. Discover what really is, because in that is truth and beauty and the happiness you seek. Thoughts can be imagined into a thousand different ego-driven plots, but if you can truly enjoy what is then you will experience real, peaceful magic.

Action: at this very moment describe what is. Invite in the understanding that the complexities that you may perceive don't exist.

35. MEDITATE

The silent, still times when you're left to your own devices and your inner world gets louder are the moments that your understanding goes layers deeper. You'll realise the time spent with yourself is the most crucial relationship you'll ever have in this lifetime. Strengthening that relationship is done in solitude.

Action: meditate for 20 minutes today.

36. TRIUMPH WITH PERSISTENCE

There's no long-term comfort in comfort; it's a place of stagnant lack. Abundance occurs in uncomfortable times, which provide your biggest challenge. Hold in your heart a sense of assurance that hard days are given so you become better. Your reason why and purpose are the greatest motivators to get you through the good and not so good days.

Action: boil the kettle and enjoy a cosy herbal tea. Write down the latest hurdle you overcame and what growth you experienced from it.

About the author

Holistic wellness expert Ali Oetjen is committed to guiding individuals towards their highest potential. She seemlessly merges her expertise in meditation, breathwork, yoga, neurolinguistic programming and therapy to enhance her clients' well-being. Through her company Ali Wellness she offers tailored one-on-one coaching, immersive retreats and self-discovery workshops as well as a meditation and breathwork subscription service that shares her wisdom worldwide. Despite her TV celebrity years Ali has returned to her true purpose: inspiring people to elevate global consciousness and embrace their best selves.

alioetjen | Alioetjen.com

About the illustrator

Marion Piret, alias Illustre Mayon, is a digital illustrator based in Rennes, France. Inspired by women, yoga, self-love and the universe, she creates peaceful and inspirational illustrations. Her aim is to bring some magic to people's lives through her art to empower and make every woman feel at peace with herself.

Illustremayon | Illustremayon.com

ROCKPOOL